Legal & Disclaimer

The information contained in this book and its contents is not designed to replace nor take the place of any form of medical or professional advice; it is not meant to replace the need for independent medical, financial, legal, or other professional advice or services, as may be required. The content and information in this book have been provided for educational and entertainment purposes only.

The content and information contained in this book have been compiled from sources deemed reliable, and they are accurate to the best of the author's knowledge, information, and beliefs. However, the author cannot guarantee its accuracy and validity and cannot be held liable for any errors and/or omissions. Furthermore, changes are periodically made to this book as and when needed. Where appropriate and/or necessary, you must consult a professional (including but not limited to your doctor, attorney, financial advisor, or other professional advisors) before using any of the suggested remedies, techniques, or information in this book.

Upon using the contents and information contained in this book, you agree to hold harmless the author from and against any damages, costs, and expenses, including any legal fees potentially resulting from the application of any of the information provided by this book. This disclaimer applies to any loss, damages or injury caused by the use and application, whether directly or indirectly, of any advice or information presented, whether for breach of contract, tort, negligence, personal injury, criminal intent, or under any other cause of action.

Table of Contents

Introduction

We all have the same 24 hours in a day. However, why is it that some people seem to get so many things done effortlessly while others are struggling? Worst still, many people have no idea where to start or what to do, and before you know it, the day has passed without anything to show for it.

Whether you are an office worker, entrepreneur, student, or homemaker - wouldn't it be great if you can get more things done in a timely manner? On a typical day, are your thoughts all over the place? Do you often miss deadlines and put off important tasks? Are you easily distracted by your social media updates, phone calls, and texts? If your answer is yes, you are not alone as a lack of focus is a common problem that affects millions of people.

We already know qualities like passion, discipline, tenacity, integrity, and ambition are what it takes to be successful in life. However, what truly separates successful individuals from the rest is their ability to **laser focus** versus those who can only concentrate for a few minutes because they lose attention to every distraction. Simply put, without a focused mindset, we cannot think effectively, follow-through our commitments, be productive, or pay attention to important information that will help achieve our goals.

The good news is that this book will show you how to develop a focused mindset quickly. By following the step-by-step techniques and tips given in this book, you can expect yourself to be operating at peak performance no matter what you are doing. After all, don't you agree that your life will be significantly enhanced if you are more productive, finish projects and tasks on time, make good and fast decisions with clarity, and be more present when spending time with family and friends?

Chapter 1 - Why You Can't Focus

"You become what you give your attention to." -Epictetus

Every day you have to rely on your ability to focus on getting your work and tasks done. However, some days you can't seem to get your never-ending to-do list done because you simply cannot focus on anything for more than a few minutes. When you cannot focus, you lose your attention and can't think clearly or focus on the task at hand; this, in return, impacts your work performance and decision-making ability. You know the familiar feeling of needing to get some things done urgently, but your attention span just won't cooperate because every noise or distraction draws it further away. What is happening?

Common signs of lack of focus:

- Restlessness and difficulty in sitting still.

- Lack of clear thinking.

- Inability to make decisions.

- Making careless mistakes.

- Inability to do complicated tasks.

- Lack of mental and physical energy to concentrate.

- Frequently forgetting things that just happened.

Lack of focus is a common problem everywhere. Studies have shown that in the U.S., an average office worker is interrupted every 3 to 10 minutes by emails, phone calls, and colleagues. It translates to 44 percent of the time and a whopping $650 billion annually in productivity, which means a lot of unnecessary distractions are getting in the way of productivity.

According to the NeuroLeadership Institute, the human brain can focus up to 2 hours with a 20 to 30 minutes break. However, since your brain is often overloaded with sensory information, it has to prioritize; otherwise, too much focus can lead to exhaustion and weaken the focus circuits in the brain. In short, only the most relevant and interesting data gets retained while the rest are ignored. Now, there are 4 types of attention you use:

1) Selective attention

The ability to focus on one thing while tuning out the surroundings, e.g., you are at a noisy party, and you have to tune out the noise to focus on another person's voice.

2) Divided attention

The ability to manage and process multiple sources of information simultaneously, also known as multitasking, e.g., talking on the phone while doing your laundry.

3) Alternating attention

The ability to shift your focus back and forth between tasks that need different cognitive requirements, e.g., reading, and learning the recipe of a cake while doing the tasks of baking a cake.

4) Sustained attention

The ability to focus on one specific task or activity over a prolonged time, e.g., playing a video game or reading. During this time, your brain will sort out and reroute important information so that it moves up to the thinking process for deeper concentration while filtering out distractions.

Now, you might be relieved to know that it is human nature to lose focus. Science explains that losing focus is part of our human survival system, so whenever your brain notices something that requires its attention, e.g., something urgent or dangerous - it will break concentration. The downside is once your focus is broken, it will take up to 25 minutes to re-focus on your earlier task. The worst part is, it usually isn't anything important, like a redundant email that derailed you from your focus.

6 Common Reasons Why You Can't Focus:

1) Mental and physical fatigue

People often overlook that having prolonged focus requires energy; this is because your brain needs energy or rather glucose from the foods you consume to function properly. On top of that, insufficient sleep, lack of exercise, and a sedentary lifestyle can cause low energy levels, which means your brain will not function optimally. If you are often yawning at work or when studying, it means you are tired, and this impedes your ability to focus. According to a study by the University of Pennsylvania, School of Medicine, sleep deprivation can lead to impaired cognitive speed and working memory. In short, low energy level equates a lesser ability to focus.

2) Emotional stress

Your emotional state can affect your level of focus. In particular, negative emotions, such as when you are feeling angry, stressed, worried, sad, or anxious. If you are prone to worry or view every negative news as severe or threatening, it will cause your mood to tank. It will be impossible for you to focus on anything because your mind is so preoccupied with your emotions. On the other hand, good or exciting news can also cause distraction, e.g., you won the lottery and are too excited to study for your upcoming exams. As you can see, not keeping your emotions in check can affect your focus.

3) Lack of planning

Do you wake up knowing what you are supposed to do for the day? Sometimes the lack of focus is due to lack of direction or purpose. It is much easier to focus when you plan ahead and know what you are supposed to be doing for the day. Imagine going to the supermarket without a shopping list. It will probably take you much longer because your attention is now drawn to numerous items along the aisle versus a quick fifteen-minute trip had you come prepared with a list.

4) Lack of interest

It is tough to concentrate on something you find boring, and you will even find ways to put it off, e.g., shopping online instead of writing your report or studying. On the other hand, if it is something you are keen on such as the latest Star Wars movie, you will not waste time attending to it. Similarly, when you are interested in your work, it is much easier to focus and be engaged by the task. Sometimes the lack of focus is simply procrastination in disguise.

5) Interruptions

Have you tried to concentrate on something, only to be interrupted by your colleagues, family members, pets, etc.? It is hard to concentrate when people are interrupting you constantly.

6) Digital distraction

Are you constantly checking your phone for social media updates, such as Facebook, Twitter, and Instagram? According to a report by Forbes, there is no proof that social media can reduce our attention span permanently. However, overuse of social media can accustom your brain to operate over a short timescale. If you are constantly distracted by your screen time, you will find it difficult to focus on your work.

Now that you are familiar with the six biggest culprits causing you to lose focus on any given day, let's move on to how having a focused mindset will positively improve your life.

Chapter 2 - How a Focused Mindset will Positively Change Your Life

"Life is like a camera. Focus on what's important, and you will capture it perfectly." -Anonymous

J.S. Bach, who was voted the greatest composer of all time by BBC Music Magazine, composed an incredible 1128 pieces of music during his lifetime of 65 years. Can you imagine the kind of laser focus Bach had to be able to produce so many pieces? Even if you are not an aspiring musician, writer, or artist, you will still stand to gain in life with a focused mindset if you apply it to everything you do.

1) **Improved memory**

Have you ever forgotten someone's name, just moments after you've met them? Well, the reason why you forget new information so quickly is that you were not paying attention. The best way to retain information is through your ability to focus. Imagine being able to retain and process new information because you could ignore distractions and concentrate on committing the details to memory - no more embarrassing moments of forgetting someone's name.

2) **Improved decisiveness**

Imagine not second-guessing yourself, overanalyzing every decision, or asking others for their opinions. Instead, you can focus on the issue at hand and evaluate your circumstances by considering the various options. Decisiveness is a crucial skill not only for leaders but for a life-changing skill that:

- Saves you time, energy, and even money from going back and forth.

- Results in faster decision-making bringing about quicker results.

- Improves productivity by not slowing down work.

- Reduces procrastination.

- Boosts confidence because you are the leader of your own life.

3) **Increased productivity**

When you are in a state of flow, you can ignore distractions and stay on task. During this time, you focus by blocking all external stimuli that might derail your momentum, and, instead, set your attention entirely on the task at hand. The result is greater productivity and higher quality work done in less time. In short, you will:

- Do more in less time.

- Increases your earning potential at work.

- Be less stressed and more relaxed because you are on top of things.

- Have more time to do the things you enjoy or spend time with your loved ones.

4) **Better relationships**

Wives often complain that their husbands do not listen to what they are saying. Well, researchers in Chicago found that men only listen with half their brain versus women who use both sides. It does not mean that women are better listeners, but rather men and women use their brains differently. In the most likelihood, your spouse has a short attention span, and at that moment, is juggling several distractions to pay attention to what you are saying. One of the best gifts is to have someone's undivided attention. Yet, we so often do this to the people we love and value all because we spread ourselves too thin, have too little time or energy. If you want your relationships to flourish, start paying attention, and you will find yourself more present with them and enjoy a better connection, improved intimacy, and trust.

5) Grit

Grit or mental toughness means having the passion and perseverance to achieve your goals in life. Having grit boils down to the habit of knowing what you are supposed to do consistently, your dedication to follow through, and overcome challenges and distractions repeatedly. Grit demands laser focus because you have to direct your attention to confronting challenges during any given day, but its rewards are surpassing:

- Helps you to keep going and overcome challenges to achieve success.

- Keeps you from wallowing in self-pity when you are tested.

- Focus means you are in control of your emotions and committed to what you do.

- You get your priorities right and ignore distractions.

- You have the capacity to boost the power of positive thinking and let your mind work for you.

6) Improved self-confidence

Thanks to the earlier 5 benefits we have covered, you will naturally have increased self-confidence. You will feel like you can accomplish anything because you have grit, increased productivity, better decision-making ability, improved memory, and strong relationships to back you.

Chapter 3 - Goal Setting For Success

"You get what you focus on. So focus on what you want." -
Anonymous

Your mind is a very powerful tool, and what you focus on will flourish. Imagine shooting an arrow without any target - where would you aim? If you want your goals to turn into reality, you must keep your thoughts on what you want and give your mind a sense of direction to focus on. A focused mind will aid you, whereas an unfocused mind that is unruly and cluttered with scattered thoughts will derail you from your goals. One of the things people often overlook is the importance of goal setting, which is essentially your roadmap to success. The process of goal setting will help you:

- Think about your future - short-term and long-term goals.

- Give yourself mental boundaries, which automatically keep distractions away.

- Clarify the steps you need to take to achieve your goals.

- Focus your efforts, time, and resources on essential things.

- Measure your forward progress to raise your self-confidence.

- Motivate yourself to turn your goals into reality.

Goal Setting for Success

a) **Prioritize**

Your mind cannot focus when it does not have clarity on the outcome you want to achieve. Therefore, identify which area of your life you want to work on first, e.g., career, studies, health, or relationship but not all of them at once.

b) **S.M.A.R.T**

Setting goals will guide your mind to hyper-focus and have a sense of direction of where you want to go. Your goals should contain meaning, value, and importance that motivate you to move forward. For this use S.M.A.R.T to guide you:

S = Specific

Your goals must be clear and well-defined for you to know the necessary steps toward them.

M = Measurable

Use proof to show your progress by setting up milestones, such as amounts, dates, or percentages. The milestones are there to remind you to celebrate your achievements.

A = Attainable

Your goals should be attainable and realistic based on your current state, mindset, experience, skills, and credentials. Otherwise, you might feel discouraged. If you are not at that level yet, set your goals to the preliminary stage before raising the bar.

R = Relevant

Your goals should be relevant to your life. Ask yourself if it is aligned with your values, overall objectives, and long-term goals.

T = Time-bound

Your goal must have a time frame; this will give you a sense of urgency and motivate you to prioritize your daily affairs.

Place your S.M.A.R.T goals in a few visible places, such as your mirror, desk, or refrigerator to remind yourself daily what you need to focus on.

Chapter 4 - The Truth about Multitasking

"Focus. Otherwise, you will find life becomes a blur." -Anonymous

Many people think multitasking is an impressive skill because it seems like they are being productive and saving time. Unfortunately, most people do not realize multitasking only works when you are pairing tasks that do not require much of your brainpower, e.g., talking on the phone while folding the laundry, or driving while listening to the radio. On the flip side, multitasking fails when you try to accomplish more than two dissimilar tasks that require your attention, consideration, and processing of information. For example, reading and watching TV at the same time will probably leave you unable to recall elements of the book or TV accurately. It is because your brain is not equipped for multitasking with multiple tasks that require brainpower. Your short-term memory can only store 5 to 9 things simultaneously, and whatever is not stored will be located to your long-term memory for future recall. In short, if you can't recall it, then you can't use it. So, the next time your child claims that he can study while watching TV simultaneously, turn off the TV and your child will learn to concentrate, which will not only help him study better but serve him well in life.

- Research has shown that multitasking makes you less productive by as much as 40 percent because of the brief mental blocks created in-between switching tasks. Not surprisingly, this also lowers the quality of your work and wastes time because you make more mistakes when your mind is divided.

- A study by the University of Sussex found that constant multitasking can damage your brain. People who regularly do so showed lower density in the region of their brain responsible for cognitive and emotional control.

- Multitasking impedes your ability to remember what you were doing, so you may not learn as much or have the ability to digest new concepts or information.

- A study by the University of California showed that multitasking could cause anxiety because you have to divide your attention constantly. The test showed multi-taskers exhibited higher heart rate compared to single-taskers who are far more stress-free.

- According to Forbes, only 2 percent of the population are good at multitasking, while the remaining 98 percent do not do well at all.

In a nutshell, the value of multitasking is overrated unless you are doing tasks that require little brainpower. If you are a habitual multi-tasker, it is probably one of the problems why you cannot focus for more than a few minutes without being distracted. The best way forward is to focus on a single task from start to finish. By doing so, it will improve your productivity, quality of work, conserve energy, and time, improve your attention span, and make you happier because you are not busy all the time.

Chapter 5 - Keeping Distractions at Bay

"Starve your distractions. Feed your focus." -Anonymous

Our modern world is a constant feed of distractions because of email, social media, and electronic devices, which is accessible from everywhere. If you aren't checking your phone every few minutes, you worry that you are missing out on something important. Before you know it, you have wasted an hour scrolling through the internet. When you habitually live a distracted life, it will impede your ability to focus and accomplish things. Can you recall the last time you focused on a single task for 15 minutes without any distractions? Are you ready to take back control and reclaim your focus?

10 Ways to Beat Distractions and Stay Focused

1) Every morning do the three most important and difficult tasks first, this will free up your time to be more focused and productive throughout the day.

2) Arrive at work an hour earlier before everyone else, and it will give you a head start without any distractions and beat the morning rush traffic.

3) Make your workplace an optimal space to focus and get productive by cleaning up your desk so that you minimize visual distractions such as clutter or dirt.

4) You will focus better without any background noise such as the TV or radio. They are more distracting than you realize.

5) Whenever you feel distracted, take a short break to help clear your mind.

6) Go offline until you have finished your work. Otherwise, use the internet sparingly and only for work. Alternatively, use apps such as

RescueTime, Anti-Social, Slife, and ManicTime to help you block timewaster sites on your computer.

7) Switch off your phone's notifications or put it on 'Do Not Disturb' so that it won't distract you. It will also minimize the temptation to check on texts, emails, tweets, and other social media.

8) Research shows that it takes an average of 90 minutes to accomplish a complex task. Therefore, set an undisturbed timeframe of 90 minutes to allow yourself to be in the flow state and take a break when the time is up.

9) Give yourself a shorter timeframe to work. Parkinson's Law dictates that if you give yourself 'too much time' to get the work done, you will not push very hard and will likely fill it with distractions, e.g., online shopping, or YouTube. On the other hand, if you have a tight deadline to get the work done, you will laser focus and figure a way out pronto.

10) Close the door or instruct others or colleagues that you are busy and request that they do not disturb you for a specified period. You will focus much better and get more work done without interruptions.

Chapter 6 - Foods that Impede Your Focus

"A full belly makes a dull brain. The muses starve in a cook's shop" -
Benjamin Franklin

Do you sometimes feel sleepy after your lunch hour or experience a food coma after consuming a large meal? You feel so lethargic, foggy, and sleepy that you want to take a nap. Science explains that eating a meal high in fat or carbohydrates, e.g., Thanksgiving meals take a lot of energy to digest along with elevated blood sugar, and hormones causing you to feel relaxed and lazy.

Although your brain weighs only 2 percent of your body weight, it requires 20 percent of the energy produced by your body for its function. As mentioned earlier, when your brain is not fuel with proper nutrients, it cannot maintain focus and concentration throughout your day. Furthermore, certain foods can also negatively impair your energy levels and ability to focus. According to a report by RMIT University, this is what happens to your brain when you eat unhealthy foods:

- Fats and sugars, which are high in junk foods, can cause neuroinflammation and damage the brain cells called neurons and the hippocampus, which is responsible for your memory function and processing of information.

- Junk food reduces neuroplasticity and shrinks your brain's learning capabilities as it impairs your hippocampus, which is essential for forming new memories and learning new things.

- Junk food releases the chemical dopamine in your brain, which is a reward system. When your brain is overwhelmed by dopamine, it craves more of the 'rewarding' food, thus making you crave more junk foods.

The good news is that by avoiding the foods listed below, you can avoid that tanking sensation after a meal, keep your mental focus sharp and your energy level high throughout the day:

1) **Sugary drinks,** e.g., sodas, energy drinks, milkshakes, and fruit juice. Just one can of energy drink contains as much as 16 teaspoons of sugar. Studies have shown that sugary drinks cause insulin resistance in your brain, thus impairing your brain's memory, function, learning, and neurons.

2) **Processed foods**, e.g., fast foods, fried foods, processed meats, and microwave meals, are stripped of nutrients and high in calories, fats, salt, and sugar. Research has found that consuming processed foods leads to an increase in fat or visceral fat that is associated with brain tissue damage, as well as lower levels of sugar metabolism in your brain and decreased brain tissue. Other studies also showed impaired learning ability and negative changes to your brain plasticity.

3) **Refined carbohydrates** contain highly processed grains or sugars, e.g., cereals, white bread, pasta, and pizza. These foods generally have a high glycemic index (GI) of more than 70, which means your body digests it too quickly, thus causing a spike in your blood sugar and insulin levels. Research has shown that over time high GI foods can impair brain function and memory.

4) **Trans Fats,** also known as partially hydrogenated oils, is one of the worst types of fat because it increases your bad cholesterol (LDL) and decreases your good cholesterol (HDL), thus increasing the risk of heart disease. Furthermore, studies have also shown that regular consumption of trans fats increases inflammation in your brain, thus increasing a person's risk of Alzheimer's disease, lower cognitive abilities, smaller brains, poorer memory, and recognition skills. Trans fats are often found in baked goods, fried foods, snacks, and frozen foods.

5) **Aspartame** is an artificial sweetener found in sugar-free foods. Many people who try to cut down on sugars opt for sugar-free drinks or snacks that contain artificial sweeteners. What most do not realize is that regular consumption of artificial sweeteners can result in an imbalance in antioxidants in the brain with detrimental side effects:

- Impaired cognitive capacity

- Dementia

- Depression

- Brain damage

- Irritation

- Stroke

Avoid the worst artificial sweeteners such as aspartame, sucralose, saccharin, and acesulfame K. These are found in candies, kids chewable vitamins, yogurt, cereals, nicotine gum, toothpaste, mouthwash, alcoholic drinks, cough syrup, and chewing gum, etc. Instead, opt for safer ones such as stevia, erythritol, xylitol, and yacon syrup.

Now, let's look at how you can eat your way to better focus and concentration by fueling your brain with more brainpower foods.

1) **Fatty fish,** e.g., salmon, sardines, and trout that are rich in omega 3, are known to be essential for learning and memory as well as building brain and nerve cells; this is because your brain is 60 percent fat and 50 percent of that fat is omega 3 type.

2) **Berries** are rich in antioxidants and anti-inflammatory properties, which help prevent inflammation and oxidative stress linked to brain deterioration and neurodegenerative disease. Studies have found that regular consumption of berries helps improve communication

between brain cells, thus leading to improved memory and a decrease in short-term memory loss.

3) **Coffee** contains antioxidants and caffeine, which are both brain-boosting properties that:

- Increases alertness and concentration by blocking adenosine which is a chemical messenger that makes you sleepy

- Improves mood by increasing serotonin, a 'feel-good' neurotransmitter

A study has shown that the best way to drink coffee is one large cup in the morning, followed by smaller quantities throughout the day to maintain your concentration.

4) **Dark Chocolates or cocoa powder** at 70 percent and above contain chockfull of brain-boosting compounds such as theobromine - a powerful antioxidant – caffeine and flavonoids that help boost your learning ability, memory, and delay age-related mental decline.

5) **Nuts,** especially walnuts, which also have omega 3, contain healthy fats, vitamin E, and antioxidants that are all beneficial to brain health.

6) **Pumpkin seeds** can be easily consumed as a healthy snack or added to salads. They contain powerful antioxidants that help protect your brain from free radical damage. Furthermore, they also contain:

- Iron, which helps prevent brain fog and impaired brain function

- Zinc, which is critical for nerve signaling, and having a zinc deficiency has been linked to neurological conditions such as Alzheimer's and Parkinson's disease

- Copper, which is used by our brain to control nerve signals

- Magnesium, which is essential for our learning and memory

7) **Eggs** contain choline in their yolks, and studies have found that higher choline intake can improve your memory and mental function.

8) **Oranges, strawberries, guava, kiwi, bell peppers, and tomatoes** contain vitamin C, which is a powerful antioxidant that is important for preventing mental decline as it helps fight off free radicals that damage our brain cells.

9) **Turmeric** is a yellow spice found in curry powder and can be consumed as turmeric tea. Its active ingredient is curcumin, which contains powerful antioxidant and anti-inflammatory properties known to improve memory and boost brain cell growth.

10) Water

Did you know that your brain is 80 percent water, and your entire body is made up of 60-70 percent water? Even mild dehydration at 2 percent can impair your brain function and energy levels. Many people do not realize that staying hydrated adequately is crucial for our overall health, especially our brain because it helps:

- Boosts concentration levels by making us more alert and attentive

- Maintains memory functions making it easier to memorize and recall information

- Improves cognition and problem-solving skills

- Increases blood flow and oxygen to the brain

- Improves reaction time by 14 percent

- Balances moods and emotions as dehydration can bring our mood down

- Lessens stress by reducing cortisone levels and anxiety

- Prevents headaches and migraines caused by dehydration as little as 2 percent

Aim to drink at least 8 cups of water daily to maintain your brain's focus and performance.

Chapter 7 - Creating a Focused Mindset Environment

Your environment plays a big part in how well you can focus. A conducive environment will help you to avoid distractions and be in a flow state of deep focus, whereas an unsupportive environment will make it impossible for you to maintain your attention for long. Simply put, merely by tweaking your environment, you will be surprised at how easily you can zero in on your work and get things done efficiently.

Creating an Environment that Maximizes Your Ability to Focus

1) Lighting

Studies have shown that people who work in a well-lit environment focus better, are more mentally engaged and happier. On the other hand, dim light, such as those in some offices, can negatively affect your focus and productivity. It also explains why people tend to feel more sluggish during the winter months when there is less daylight. Natural lighting is the most ideal because it delivers warmth and vitality in a room. If you don't have access to natural lighting, make sure there is sufficient light. Do not underestimate the effect of lighting on your ability to focus. Otherwise, you might find yourself staring into space after 30 minutes.

2) Clutter

Did you know the better organized you are, the better you can focus? A clean and uncluttered workspace enables you to mentally breathe, whereas a cluttered one will distract you and hamper your ability to focus.

Suggestions:

- Remove furniture you do not need so that it gives you more mental space.

- Use only one tray for all incoming items.

- Remove all non-work items, e.g., ornaments, magazines, and books.

- Organize your desk, drawers, and stationery so that you know where to find your stapler and paper clips, etc.

- Keep cables out of sight by using cable management kits or clamps.

- Instead of a filing cabinet, switch to using cloud services, e.g., Dropbox or Google Drive, and you will clear more physical space.

3) **Comfort**

If you are not comfortable, it will affect your ability to focus and how long you can maintain your focus. Check the following:

- How comfortable are your clothes and shoes?

- The height, armrest, and back support of your chair.

- The height of your desk, e.g., can your arms form a 90-degree angle at the elbows?

- The distance of your monitor to your eyes should ideally measure 24 to 36 inches and be the same level as your sightline.

- Your sitting posture, e.g., is your back straight and shoulders back?

- Do you often sit for a long time without moving? Try to stretch every 30 minutes to relieve tension in your neck and shoulders.

4) **Temperature**

A survey revealed that 42 percent of office workers in the U.S. found their office too warm, while 56 percent found it too cold. If the room is too warm, you might fall asleep. If it is too cold, you will feel too uncomfortable. Either way, it is hard to concentrate and get things done when you are so distracted by the temperature. According to a study by Cornell University, the ideal temperature for concentration and productivity is 72 to 77°F (22 to 25°C). When set within this temperature, workers were more productive and made fewer errors at 10 percent. However, productivity dropped, and the error rate went up to 25 percent when the temperature became too cold or warm. If you can't control the thermostat, e.g., your office building, you can always:

- Dress in layers or bring a sweater or scarf if it is too cold

- Bring a small USB fan or floor fan if it is too warm

- Switch to LED bulbs which is cooler than the regular incandescent bulb

- Open a window if possible.

5) External noise

It is human nature to 'eavesdrop' or overhear others talking around us even if you don't mean to. What can you do when you are surrounded by colleagues who are discussing non-work related things, e.g., where to eat for lunch?

- Wear your noise-canceling headphones.

- Move to another location.

- Take the chance to have a break outside, and hopefully, the conversation is over by the time you return.

- If you are working at home, ask your family members to avoid disturbing you for a set period.

6) **Scents**

Did you know that certain scents can improve your focus, alertness, mood, and productivity? If you can't use scented candles, diffusers, or scented oils at your workplace, you can dab some essential oil into a small towel or handkerchief to inhale periodically. If you work at home or can use scents liberally, here are some recommended ones for focus and productivity:

- Peppermint

- Spearmint

- Rosemary

- Lemon

- Jasmine

- Cinnamon

- Basil

- Lavender

Chapter 8 - 10 Techniques for Laser Beam Focus

"The successful warrior is the average man, with laser-like focus." - *Bruce Lee*

1) Specify your purpose

One of the reasons why you become distracted easily is because you do not know your real purpose for doing something. For example, you need to study for an exam, and you want to score well. Studying is a serious business because it means hours of focused time. However, the moment you see all the notes you have to memorize, you find it so dreary that you can't concentrate and become distracted by your phone, friends, and all things unrelated. You see, whenever your brain finds the task at hand monotonous, it will automatically seek out distractions. To counter this, you need to remind yourself how your grades will affect your future; this will give your brain clarity of purpose so that it knows you mean business and to stop putting up internal resistance that hampers your progress.

2) Use a timer

Earlier, we discussed Parkinson's Law and giving yourself a shorter timeframe to complete a task. Now go one step further by using a timer on your desk to set up self-imposed deadlines for *all* your tasks. For example, you need to prepare a report for your boss, and you know from experience it usually takes you 2 hours. Therefore, set your timer for 2 hours. The visual sight of the timer counting down before you will spur you to take action. It will keep you focused, motivated, and less inclined to procrastination and distractions because you know time is running out.

Tip: Use a kitchen timer instead of your phone as apps can pose distractions.

3) Less is more

The less you have on your plate, the easier you can focus on your tasks. Limit your to-do list to the 5 most important tasks. If your list is too long at 10-15, you will be playing catch-up and feeling distracted by the uncompleted tasks waiting for you. Having a shorter to-do list means you can focus on the important tasks and complete them on time without compromising on the quality. At the same time, it also helps you to make it a habit to identify and remove unimportant and non-essential tasks so that you can focus on the most important tasks every day.

4) Single-tasking

You now have an idea of why multitasking does not work and that it can make you more prone to distractions affecting your productivity. Imagine talking to someone on the phone while they were too distracted multitasking, e.g., they were checking emails on the phone? No doubt, you will find it frustrating not to have their undivided attention or meaningful contribution to the conversation. Today, commit yourself to the habit of single-tasking. Pick one important task, turn off all other distractions, e.g., phones, emails, and give it your full focus for an allocated time. Once completed, repeat with the next task on your list. If you keep doing this, it will become a new habit that serves you well.

Tip: Practice being focused on the person you are talking to and give them your full attention.

5) Well-timed breaks

Taking well-timed breaks will help you maintain focus, improve productivity, and prevent burnout. Researchers from the University of Illinois found that subjects who worked on a focus intensive task for 50 minutes scored the highest on mental stamina. The conclusion is, most people work better on a recommended break of 15 to 20 minutes for every 50 to 90 minutes of work to maintain focus and productivity. You can also follow the Pomodoro technique, which recommends 25 minutes, followed by a 3 to 5 minute break or 90 minutes, followed by a 15 to 30 minute break. During your break, stay away from screen time, including your phone. Do some stretching, take a walk, or have a coffee break.

6) Exercise

Many studies prove that exercise is essential for improving your brain health. When you exercise, it increases oxygen to your brain, thus reducing memory fog while boosting brain growth and forging new neuron connections. The best form of exercise for your brain is blood pumping ones, such as aerobic exercises, running, cycling, or exercise that requires hand-eye coordination or motor skills, e.g., tennis, which helps brain building.

Tip: If you want to remain mentally sharp throughout the day, do your exercise in the morning.

7) Identify common distractions

Many of your distractions are probably common ones that happen frequently. By identifying and addressing these triggers, you can prevent them from spiraling out of control, e.g., you always get peckish in the afternoon; this distracts you from your work as you hunt down for a snack to satisfy your cravings. Now that you have identified this as a trigger prepare beforehand a granola bar or nuts for when you start to feel peckish; this will minimize your downtime. Another example could be that you often feel sleepy right after lunch hour and cannot concentrate on your work. The solution could be opting for a lighter lunch such as salads or soups to prevent the tanking sensation, which will rob you from focusing on your task.

8) Take a walk

Did you know that innovators like Steve Job and Mark Zuckerberg conduct walking meetings with their team to harness the best ideas? Whenever you feel distracted, go outside and take a walk. It will soothe your mental fatigue and restore your attention span. Researchers at Stanford University found that walking can improve your focus, short-term memory, and creativity. It is best to walk in nature as the fresh air will restore and lift your mood. When you return to your task, you will feel mentally refreshed, relaxed, and motivated to find creative solutions.

9) Create a daily routine

Your focus will thrive more on routine than spontaneity because your brain prefers structure. Knowing what comes next allows your brain to focus on the next action rather than being distracted by a spontaneous series of actions. Most highly productive people like Jeff Bezos, CEO of Amazon, have fixed routines, such as having 8 hours of sleep at night. He enjoys starting his mornings with a good breakfast and reading the newspapers. In the afternoons, Bezos handles top priority tasks and leaves the evenings for winding down. Take some time to think about your daily routine. By having a routine, you don't need motivation or willpower to act, as you will merely be prompted to follow through. The best part is that you can now devote more attention to your tasks and get things done more efficiently. Through repetition, your brain will learn what to expect next, and you will find it easier to manage your focus and less prone to distraction because your routine is helping you stay on track.

10) Meditation

The practice of meditation is no longer only associated with monks and mystics. It has gone mainstream, almost like a new normal for many. The best part is neuroscientists have proven the benefits of meditation. Using MRI scans showed that regular practitioners like

Zen meditators have a greater mental focus and more control over wandering thoughts than non-practitioners. Science explains that during meditation, your brain waves transit from your normal hyper-state of Gamma and Beta to slower relaxed awareness states such as Alpha and Theta. In fact, studies have shown that only 4 days of meditation can improve your memory and attention span. If you have not tried meditation before, here's a simple one to start with:

- Sit in a comfortable position with your back straight

- Set your timer for 5 min

- Gently close your eyes

- Start by inhaling slowly till your breath fills your entire body, then exhale slowly

- Repeat this breathing cycle until the 5 minutes is up

- It is normal that your mind may wander repeatedly - just bring it back gently to focus on your breathing again

- Gradually increase your practice from 5 min to 20 min as you get more comfortable

The secret to long-lasting results is consistency and patience, and in time, you will cultivate a relaxed and focused state of mind.

Chapter 9 - 7 Instant Tips for Fast Focus

"Your focus determines your reality." -Anonymous

1) Energy level

Your energy levels fluctuate throughout the day. At times you can get things done quickly, and at other times, you struggle from lack of energy. Are you an early bird or a night owl who functions best in the evenings? Learn to identify your high energy times and schedule important tasks to those hours when you are naturally more focused and alert. At the same time, schedule unimportant tasks, e.g., answering emails, and phone calls to your low energy times.

2) Music

Using the right music can help you block out external distractions and enter a state of flow. It is especially useful if you are working in the office and surrounded by conversations between your colleagues or at home when your children are around. Researchers have found that instrumental or classical music can help us get into the optimal state of flow. Find music that you like and play it on repeat when you are working.

3) Coffee

Did you know that drinking coffee at different times of the day can increase or reduce its benefits? According to experts, the best time to drink your coffee for alertness is when it works with your natural biological rhythms. For the average person who gets up at 6.00 am, their cortisol levels peaks at:

- 8 to 9 am

- 12 to 1 pm

- 5.30 to 6.30 pm

During this time, you are already naturally perky. Therefore, you do not need the extra caffeine kick. Instead, you should drink your coffee after your cortisol peak at:

- 9 to 11.30 am

- 1 to 5 pm

The next time you find yourself struggling with your task, have some well-timed coffee break to improve your focus.

4) Black tea

While coffee makes us alert, drinking tea helps us to pay more attention thus improving our memory. Black tea, e.g., English breakfast tea, contains L-theanine, an amino acid that promotes attention in the brain, thus enabling us to perform tasks better than non-tea drinkers.

5) Reward

It is especially easy to lose concentration when we find ourselves doing things that are boring or tedious. In this case, use the reward system to motivate yourself to complete the task, e.g., a slice of cake. The anticipation of a reward will offset the boredom and help you stay on course.

6) Chewing gum

A study by Cardiff University UK found that chewing gum can improve alertness, learning, memory, and intelligence. This is because chewing gum for 20 minutes increases blood flow to the brain, which acts as a warm-up for the brain. Try chewing gum the next time you need to stay alert and focus.

7) Disconnect

According to statistics, the average user's attention span for videos is 30 seconds for Instagram, 1 minute for Facebook, and 2 minutes for YouTube. The numbers are declining every year, and too much 'instant' information appears to be affecting people's attention span to a subject. As part of your re-training to focus, disconnect your phone and Wi-Fi, etc., when you are working. You will find that you are far less susceptible to distractions, and you can focus on what truly matters.

Conclusion

Thank you for reading this book and for investing time in your personal development.

As you can see, improving your focus and attention span is about making small changes in your life and being consistent. The upside is the more you practice, the easier it gets, and soon you will be getting more done in less time. The best part is that you will now have more free time with your loved ones to be able to do the things you truly love.

I would be extremely grateful if you could *post me a review and some feedback* on how this book has inspired you to want to take that much needed step to focus and more importantly, stay focused! I am already feeling excited for you as I know the moment you start to see some validation of your efforts in not wavering, you will stay true to focusing. It's that SIMPLE!

To Your Success,

Ritzy Hallmark

Checkout My Other Books

www.ingramcontent.com/pod-product-compliance
Lightning Source LLC
Chambersburg PA
CBHW030544220526
45463CB00007B/2978